WRjC

TULSA CITY-COUNTY LIBRARY

D1449923

Who Grows Up in the Rain Forest?

A Book About Rain Forest Animals and Their Offspring

Written by Theresa Longenecker
Illustrated by Melissa Carpenter

Content Advisor: Julie Dunlap, Ph.D.
Reading Advisor: Lauren A. Liang, M.A.
Literacy Education, University of Minnesota
Minneapolis, Minnesota

PICTURE WINDOW BOOKS
Minneapolis, Minnesota

Editor: Peggy Henrikson
Designer: Melissa Voda
Page production: The Design Lab
The illustrations in this book were prepared digitally.

Picture Window Books
5115 Excelsior Boulevard
Suite 232
Minneapolis, MN 55416
1-877-845-8392
www.picturewindowbooks.com

Copyright © 2003 by Picture Window Books
All rights reserved. No part of this book may be reproduced without written permission from the publisher.
The publisher takes no responsibility for the use of any of the materials or methods described in this book,
nor for the products thereof.

Printed in the United States of America.
1 2 3 4 5 6 08 07 06 05 04 03

Library of Congress Cataloging-in-Publication Data
Longenecker, Theresa, 1955–
  Who grows up in the rain forest? : a book about rain forest animals and their offspring / written by
Theresa Longenecker ; illustrated by Melissa Carpenter.
     p. cm.
  Summary: Names and describes the offspring of a jaguar, poison arrow frog, macaw, capybara, gibbon,
sloth, anteater, and boa constrictor.
  ISBN 1-4048-0027-1 (lib. bdg. : alk. paper)
  1. Rain forest animals—Infancy—Juvenile literature. [1. Rain forest animals—Infancy.] I. Carpenter,
Melissa, ill. II. Title.
  QL112 .L663 2003
  599.139—dc21
                                                                                                2002006274

J 599.139 L857wr 2003
Longenecker, Theresa, 1955-
Who grows up in the rain
forest? : a book about rain

Drip, splash, plop. It's wet here. Vines wind around tall trees. Green leaves block out the sunlight. This is the rain forest. Many baby animals grow up in the rain forest. They might live in trees, on the ground, or in water. Some baby animals stay with their parents for a while. Others survive on their own.

Let's read about some of the animals that grow up in the rain forest.

Tadpole

A baby green poison arrow frog is called a tadpole.

After the tiny tadpoles hatch, they wriggle up onto the back of the father frog. He carries them from the small pool where they hatched to a nearby stream or lake. Once they are in their new home, they will grow on their own.

Did you know?
The tadpoles won't fall off their father's back. They're stuck on with a special, sticky liquid that washes away once they reach water.

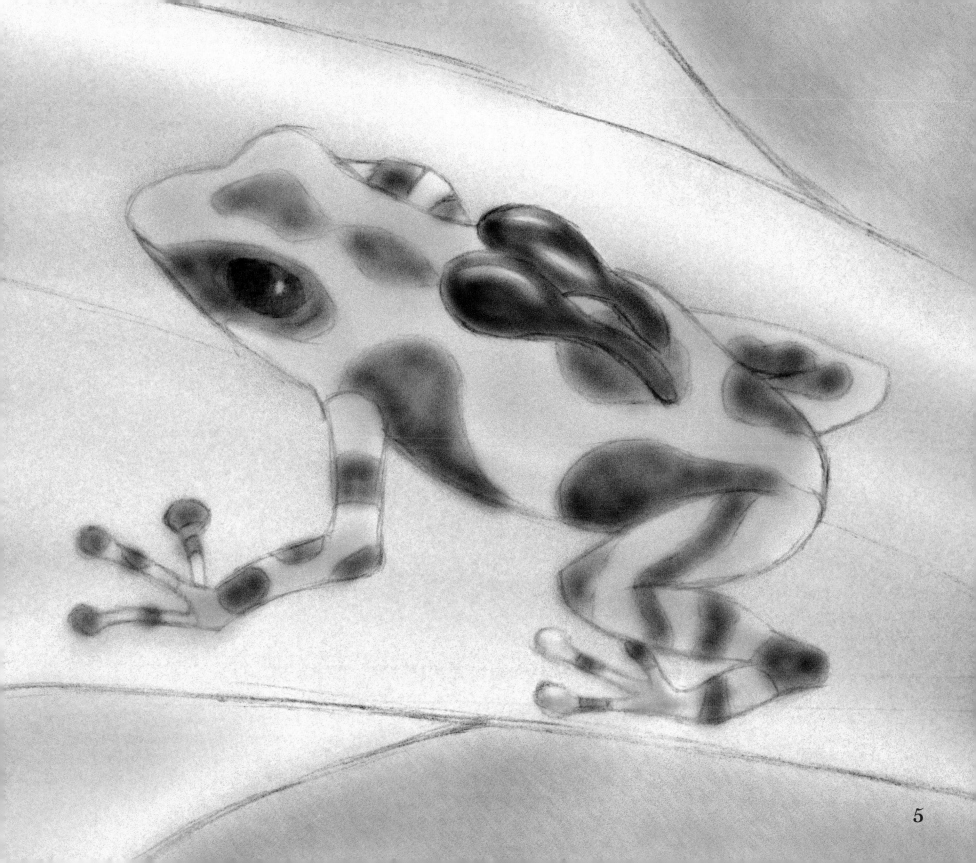

5

Chick

A baby scarlet macaw is called a chick.

When they first hatch, macaw chicks have no feathers at all. These chicks are over one month old. Their new, white feathers are just beginning to show some color.

Baby capybara

A baby capybara is called a baby capybara.

Right after birth, this baby capybara can walk and will follow its mother. It talks to her with grunts and whistles.

Did you know?
A baby capybara is born with open eyes and a full coat of fur.

Baby gibbon

A baby white-cheeked gibbon is called a baby gibbon.

Holding on tight, this little gibbon gets a ride as its mother swings through the trees. The baby was born with tan fur— the same color as its mother's.

Did you know?
During the first year, the baby's fur turns black, the color of its father. Later, young female gibbons will turn tan again and stay that color. Young males remain black.

11

Cub

A baby jaguar is called a cub.

Jaguar cubs stay near their mother when they first leave their hidden den. Playing makes them stronger. Later they will follow their mother and watch her as she hunts and fishes. The cubs learn to flip fish out of the water with their paws.

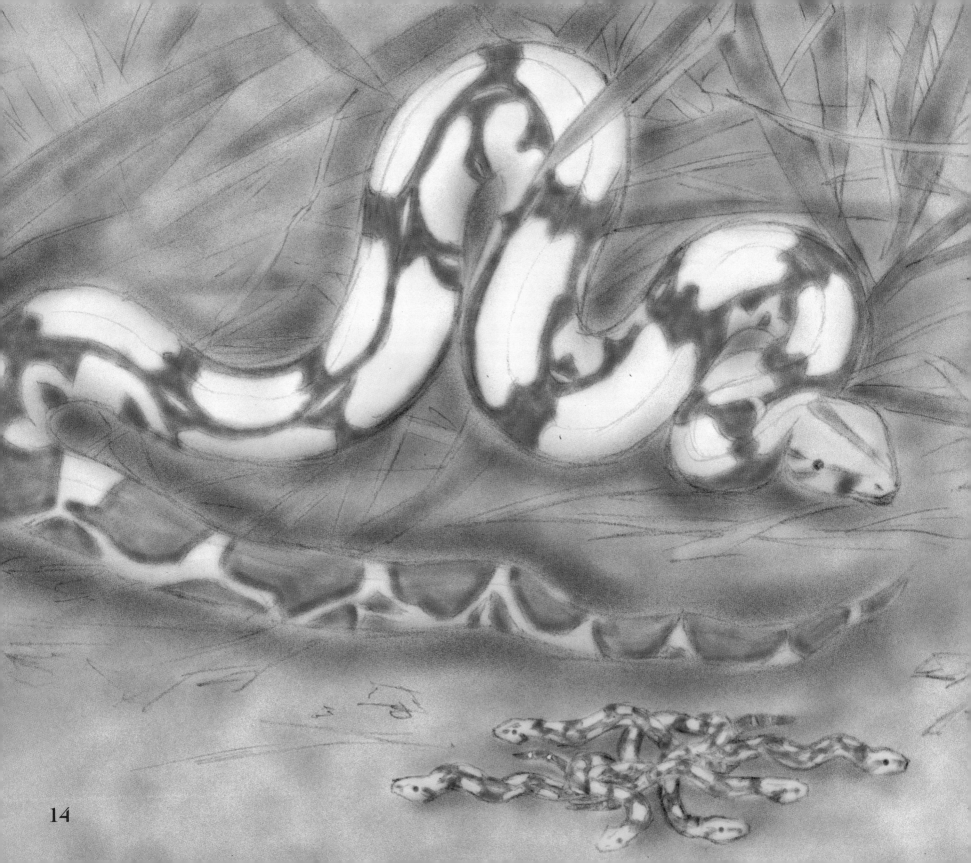

14

Hatchling

A baby Surinam redtail boa constrictor is called a hatchling.

A boa constrictor hatchling hatches with 20 to 60 other baby boas. The mother boa does not take care of the hatchlings. They are able to find food on their own.

Baby sloth

A baby three-toed sloth is called a baby sloth.

Nestling into its mother's chest, this little sloth is safe, high in the trees. The baby will cling to its mother until it is six months old.

Did you know?

A sloth moves so slowly that tiny plants grow on its fur. Soon, this baby will look greenish like its mother. Its green color will help the sloth hide among the leaves.

Baby anteater

A baby giant anteater is called a baby anteater.

Riding on its mother's back, this baby anteater is safe from harm. At night, mother and baby will both rest under the cover of the mother's huge bushy tail.

Fast Facts

Green Poison Arrow Frog: It takes several weeks for a tadpole to grow into an adult poison arrow frog. After it starts developing legs and markings, it is called a froglet. Even as an adult, the poison arrow frog is only about one and one-half inches (less than four centimeters) long. The bright colors of the adult frog warn enemies to stay away. If animals try to eat the frog, they may die from the poison in the frog's skin.

Scarlet Macaw: The female scarlet macaw lays one to four eggs at a time. Her nest is usually in a hole, high in a tree. When the chicks hatch, they are helpless. To feed them, the parents spit up nuts, fruit, and seeds that they have eaten. This makes the food easier for the chicks to eat. Later, the chicks will be strong enough to crack open nuts with their own sharp, curved beaks. They will also be able to use their feet to hold food and grasp tree branches. Scarlet macaw chicks stay with their parents for about two years.

Capybara: Capybara babies are usually born four at a time. At birth, a baby capybara weighs about two pounds (almost one kilogram). An adult can weigh over 100 pounds (45 kilograms) and is about the size of a pig. The capybara is the world's largest rodent. A baby can eat plants right away, but its mother's milk is its main food for the first several weeks. Capybaras like to stand in waterholes and eat grasses that grow along the banks. Their partly webbed feet make them good swimmers.

White-Cheeked Gibbon: A baby gibbon will stay close to its mother and drink her milk for about a year. During its second year, the young gibbon spends more time with its father. Then it begins to eat fruit, leaves, insects, and bird eggs. A young gibbon lives with its parents for six to eight years. It learns to travel in the trees. A gibbon can leap up to three car lengths in one jump.

Jaguar: Jaguar litters include one to four cubs. The cubs' eyes are closed at birth but will open in two weeks. The cubs live in their den for up to six months, and they stay with their mother for two years. Jaguars eat just about anything they can catch. They can even leap through the trees to catch monkeys.

Surinam Redtail Boa Constrictor: One to two weeks after birth, a hatchling will shed its skin for the first time. A young boa will shed its skin every month, and the snake keeps growing its whole life. A hatchling eats very small animals. A boa doesn't chew its food. The snake's jaw, throat, and body stretch so it can swallow its prey whole. After a meal, an adult boa can go without eating for weeks or months.

Three-Toed Sloth: A baby sloth's first food is its mother's milk. At about four months of age, it will begin to eat leaves and beetles. The three-toed sloth gets its name from the three toes it has on each foot. Each toe has a long, hooked claw for hanging upside down from tree branches. Sloths move so slowly and sleep so much that the word *sloth* has come to mean "lazy."

Giant Anteater: Baby anteaters are born one at a time. The baby is born with fur and all its markings. During much of the first year, it rides on its mother's back. After about four months, it begins to take short trips away from its mother. It hops back on its mother when it's scared or tired. The baby will stay with its mother for about two years before going off on its own. Anteaters can't see well. They depend on their sense of smell to hunt for ants and termites to eat.

Rain Forest Babies at a Glance

Word for Baby	Animal	Born How	First Food	Word for Group
Tadpole	Poison arrow frog	Egg	Insects, rotting plants, frog eggs	Knot
Chick	Scarlet macaw	Egg	Insects	Flock
Baby	Capybara	Live	Mother's milk	Horde
Baby	White-cheeked gibbon	Live	Mother's milk	——
Cub	Jaguar	Live	Mother's milk	——
Hatchling	Boa constrictor	Egg	Small rodents	——
Baby	Three-toed sloth	Live	Mother's milk	——
Baby	Giant anteater	Live	Mother's milk	——

Where Do They Live?

Green poison arrow frog — Central and South America, and Hawaii

Scarlet macaw — Central and South America

Capybara — South America

White-cheeked gibbon — southeastern Asia

Jaguar — southern Mexico and throughout South America

Surinam redtail boa constrictor — northeastern South America

Three-toed sloth — Central and South America

Giant anteater — Central and South America

Make a "Save the Rain Forest" Notebook

Did you know that most of the paper you use every day is made from trees? You can help save the trees in the rain forest by using less paper. This special notebook is made from paper that has already been used once.

What You Need

2 sheets of thin 8½-by-11-inch cardboard or poster board

3-hole punch

20 sheets of any kind of 8½-by-11-inch paper that have already been used on one side

String

Scissors

Crayons or markers

What to Do

1. With the 3-hole punch, punch holes along the left-hand side of each piece of cardboard.

2. Arrange the papers so that the clean sides are all facing up. If your paper doesn't have holes, use the 3-hole punch to punch holes along the left-hand side of each of your 20 sheets of paper.

3. Neatly stack the papers. Place one cardboard sheet on the top and one cardboard sheet on the bottom of your stack, matching up the holes.

4. Cut the string into three, 6-inch (15-centimeter) pieces, and tie your notebook together.

5. Using crayons or markers, decorate the cover of your notebook with drawings of baby animals from the rain forest. Admire your rain forest notebook! By using recycled paper, you are helping to save the rain forest.

Words to Know

den—a wild animal's home, usually a shallow hole or cave

litter—a group of animals born at the same time to the same mother

prey—an animal that another animal hunts for food

rodent—a furry animal with long, sharp teeth used for biting and chewing on things. Capybaras, rats, gophers, guinea pigs, and beavers are rodents.

termite—an insect that eats wood

webbed feet—feet with toes that have flaps of skin between them

To Learn More

At the Library

Bach, Julie S. *Sloths*. Mankato, Minn.:
  Creative Education, 1999.

Greenwood, Elinor. *Rain Forest*. New York:
  DK Pub., 2001.

Martin, James. *Boa Constrictors*. Minneapolis:
  Capstone Press, 1996.

Schaefer, Lola M. *Leopards: Spotted Hunters*.
  Mankato, Minn.: Bridgestone Books, 2002.

On the Web

Want to learn more about baby animals?
Visit FACT HOUND at *http://www.facthound.com*.

Index